Take-Along Guide

Tracks, Scats and Signs

by Leslie Dendy
illustrations by Linda Garrow

NORTHWORD PRESS
Minnetonka, Minnesota

CONTENTS

Tracks, Scats and Signs

THE FIELD

Grasshoppers and butterflies are easy to find in a field, but many animals are hiding. Look for paths mashed down in the grass.

Hunt for little piles of dirt. These mounds could mark the "door" to the home of a dirt-digger, like a badger or a woodchuck.

Watch ants carrying food to their nest along tiny trails. The ants can smell their way. They make trails by dotting chemicals on the ground with their tail-ends.

Look closely at the plants. You may find a funnel-shaped spider web or a pile of grass pieces chewed by a mouse.

FOXES

Finding a fox is tricky business. But you can find fox tracks trotting through a field or forest.

A fox paw print has four toes with claw marks. A fox often walks in a straight line. Its rear feet step in the same spots as its front feet. This makes a neat dotted line. If you see sloppier tracks wandering around, they probably were made by a dog.

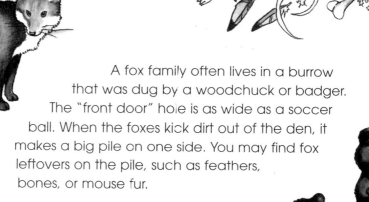

A fox family often lives in a burrow that was dug by a woodchuck or badger. The "front door" hole is as wide as a soccer ball. When the foxes kick dirt out of the den, it makes a big pile on one side. You may find fox leftovers on the pile, such as feathers, bones, or mouse fur.

SNAKES

A snake can slide between the blades of grass and sneak up on a frog. It can slither into a mouse tunnel.

How can an animal with no feet make tracks?

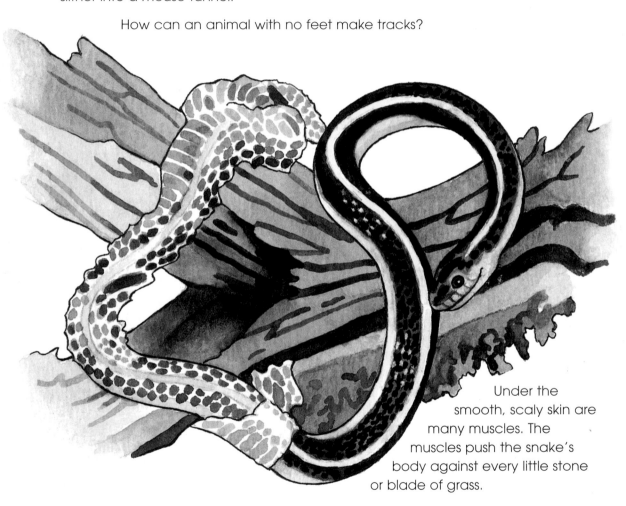

Under the smooth, scaly skin are many muscles. The muscles push the snake's body against every little stone or blade of grass.

24

The snake's whole body slithers forward and makes a curvy track.

This is tough on the snake's skin. But it can grow a new skin every few months, inside the old skin.

When it's ready to shed, the snake rubs its head on a rock or branch to tear the old skin. Then it crawls around. The old skin is peeled off, inside out. You might find it on the ground.

25

BEAVERS

Using its front teeth, a beaver can chop down a tree in three minutes! Pointy-top tree stumps tell you a beaver pond is nearby.

Beavers can make their own ponds by building a dam across a stream with logs and mud. You can see trails where the beavers dragged logs. A wide zigzag in the mud shows where a beaver's fat tail was dragging.

Beavers also pile up sticks and mud to make their lodge. The "doors" are hidden under water.

When a beaver eats, it twirls a branch in its paws like corn on the cob. It gobbles the twigs, leaves, and bark. Then it weaves the bare branch into the dam or lodge.

Beavers keep busy all winter. You can see log-drag trails in the snow, or a pile of branches sticking out of the icy pond.

After many years the beavers move away. If the old dam breaks, the water rushes out. Then a meadow grows where the pond was. But you can still see the dam and lodge poking through the grass.

MAKE TRACKS THAT LAST

Animal tracks are just holes in the ground, but you can collect them with this trick. You can fill the tracks with liquid plaster, let it harden, and take the hard "casts" home. They look just like the bottoms of animal feet. This works best for tracks in mud or soft dirt.

HERE IS WHAT YOU WILL NEED

- plaster of Paris powder—in a plastic tub or coffee can with lid
- water—in a water bottle or canteen
- 1 cup measure for plaster powder
- 1/2 cup measure for water
- container to mix plaster in
- spoon
- pocket knife or table knife
- small box

HERE IS HOW TO MAKE THE PLASTER CASTS

1 Find some tracks first. Pick out two or three of the best ones.

2 Put 1/2 cup water in the mixing container.

3 Pour 1 cup plaster powder into the water.

4 Stir with the spoon until the lumps are gone. The plaster should be about as thick as pancake batter or applesauce.

5 QUICKLY pour the plaster into the tracks. Make sure it fills up all the toe holes and claw marks.

6 Let the plaster harden at least 20 to 40 minutes, until it feels as hard as a rock. Look around for more signs while you wait.

7 The casts are still fragile. Carefully cut the dirt around them with the knife, and lift them up gently.

8 Put the casts in the box to protect them on the way home. They will get harder after several hours. You can then rinse the dirt off in the sink. A soft toothbrush helps.